I'LL TRY TO BE Nicer IF YOU TRY TO BE Smarter

DARE YOU

STAMP CO.

CIDER MILL
PRESS

www.cidermillpress.com

BOOK
PUBLISHERS

THANK YOU FOR BEING SO LAME... AND MAKING ME SEEM COOLER

DARE YOU

STAMP CO.

CIDER MILL
PRESS

www.cidermillpress.com

BOOK
PUBLISHERS

DARE YOU

STAMP CO.

CIDER MILL
PRESS

www.cidermillpress.com

BOOK
PUBLISHERS

Get Well Soon

Or don't.
Whatever.

DARE YOU

STAMP CO.

CIDER MILL
PRESS

www.cidermillpress.com

BOOK
PUBLISHERS

CIDER MILL
PRESS

www.cidermillpress.com

BOOK
PUBLISHERS

Thank You

FOR HOSTING THE WORST PARTY EVER

I had a truly awful time!

CIDER MILL
PRESS

BOOK
PUBLISHERS

www.cidermillpress.com

I LIKE GOING OUT WITH YOU

Because it shows people

I BELIEVE IN HELPING

THE LESS FORTUNATE

www.cidermillpress.com

CIDER MILL
PRESS

BOOK
PUBLISHERS

#REJECTED

DARE YOU

STAMP CO.

CIDER MILL PRESS

BOOK PUBLISHERS

www.cidermillpress.com

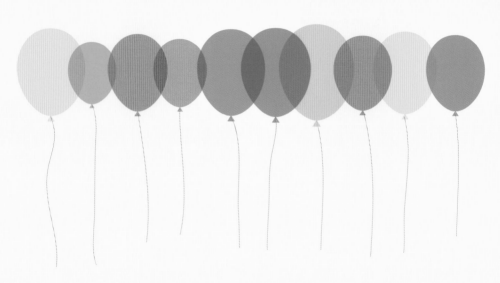

HAPPY BIRTHDAY, JERK.

DARE YOU

STAMP CO.

_____

_____

_____

_____

CIDER MILL
PRESS

www.cidermillpress.com

BOOK
PUBLISHERS

YOU SUCK

NO, REALLY

You Suck

DARE YOU

STAMP CO.

CIDER MILL
PRESS

www.cidermillpress.com

BOOK
PUBLISHERS

Just a note...

YOUR STUDENT LOAN OFFICER CALLED.

DARE YOU

STAMP CO.

CIDER MILL
PRESS

www.cidermillpress.com

BOOK
PUBLISHERS

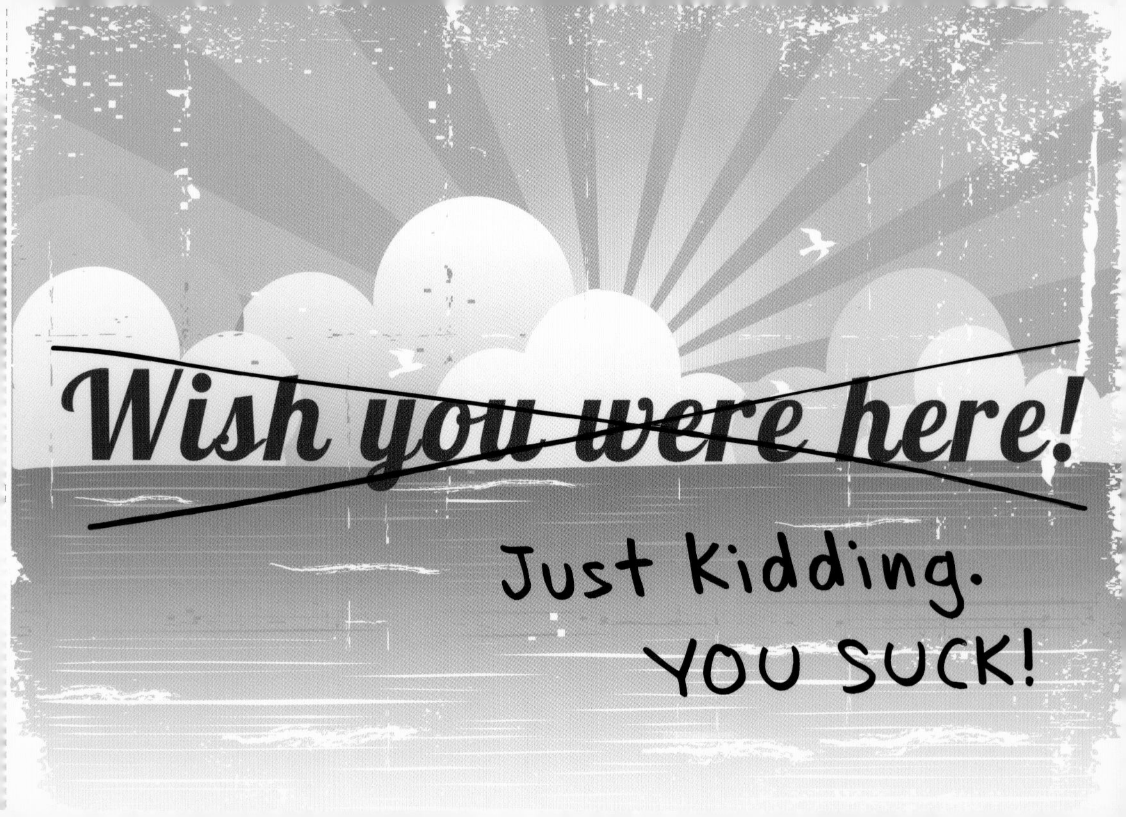
~~Wish you were here!~~
Just kidding.
YOU SUCK!

DARE YOU
STAMP CO.

CIDER MILL
PRESS

www.cidermillpress.com

BOOK
PUBLISHERS

DARE YOU

STAMP CO.

CIDER MILL
PRESS

www.cidermillpress.com

BOOK
PUBLISHERS

CIDER MILL
PRESS

BOOK
PUBLISHERS

www.cidermillpress.com

Congratulations

ON BEING LIVING PROOF
THAT EVOLUTION
CAN GO BACKWARDS

© 2015 Appleseed Press Book Publishers, LCC | Image Credit: Maximilian Laschon/Shutterstock.com

CIDER MILL
PRESS

BOOK
PUBLISHERS

www.cidermillpress.com

Happy Birthday

GREAT JOB surviving another year with that face.

DARE YOU
STAMP CO.

CIDER MILL
PRESS

www.cidermillpress.com

BOOK
PUBLISHERS

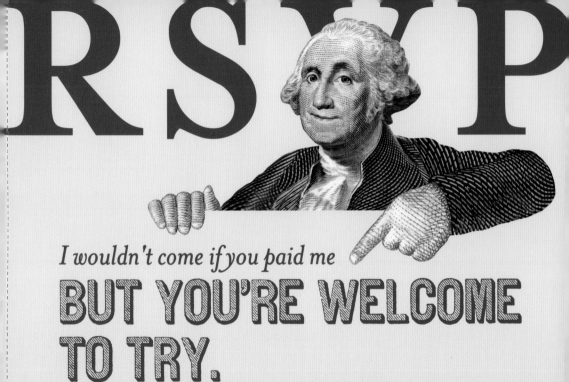

DARE YOU

STAMP CO.

CIDER MILL
PRESS

BOOK
PUBLISHERS

www.cidermillpress.com

DARE YOU
STAMP CO.

_____

_____

_____

_____

CIDER MILL
PRESS

BOOK
PUBLISHERS

www.cidermillpress.com

I'M NOT AS

STUPID

AS YOU LOOK

www.cidermillpress.com

DARE YOU

STAMP CO.

CIDER MILL
PRESS

www.cidermillpress.com

BOOK
PUBLISHERS

DARE YOU
STAMP CO.

CIDER MILL
PRESS

www.cidermillpress.com

BOOK
PUBLISHERS

YOU MUST HAVE BEEN BORN
ON THE HIGHWAY.
That's Where Most Accidents Happen.

www.cidermillpress.com

Congratulations

On accomplishing something
that literally millions of people
have already accomplished.

DARE YOU
STAMP CO.

CIDER MILL
PRESS

www.cidermillpress.com

BOOK
PUBLISHERS

You're
Invited
TO KEEP YOUR
OPINIONS
To Yourself

www.cidermillpress.com

DARE YOU

STAMP CO.

CIDER MILL
PRESS

BOOK
PUBLISHERS

www.cidermillpress.com

STAMP CO.

CIDER MILL
PRESS

BOOK
PUBLISHERS

www.cidermillpress.com

DARE YOU
STAMP CO.

CIDER MILL
PRESS

www.cidermillpress.com

BOOK
PUBLISHERS

__ YES! SO EXCITED!

__ I'LL BE THERE IN SPIRIT!

X I can't make it because
I'd rather be doing
LITERALLY anything else.

DARE YOU

STAMP CO.

CIDER MILL
PRESS

BOOK
PUBLISHERS

www.cidermillpress.com

Are you free this weekend?

*I need someone to do
my homework for me.*

DARE YOU
STAMP CO.

CIDER MILL
PRESS
BOOK
PUBLISHERS

www.cidermillpress.com